# Journey of the CARIBOU

BY BENJAMIN O. SAMUELSON

Gareth Stevens
PUBLISHING

Please visit our website, www.garethstevens.com. For a free color catalog of all our high-quality books, call toll free 1-800-542-2595 or fax 1-877-542-2596.

**Cataloging-in-Publication Data**

Names: Samuelson, Benjamin O.
Title: Journey of the caribou / Benjamin O. Samuelson.
Description: New York : Gareth Stevens Publishing, 2019. | Series: Massive animal migrations | Includes index.
Identifiers: ISBN 9781538216682 (pbk.) | ISBN 9781538216538 (library bound) | ISBN 9781538216699 (6 pack)
Subjects: LCSH: Caribou–Juvenile literature.
Classification: LCC QL737.U55 S26 2019 | DDC 599.65'8–dc23

First Edition

Published in 2019 by
**Gareth Stevens Publishing**
111 East 14th Street, Suite 349
New York, NY 10003

Copyright © 2019 Gareth Stevens Publishing

Designer: Katelyn E. Reynolds
Editor: Joan Stoltman

Photo credits: Cover, p. 1 Ingo Arndt/Minden Pictures/Getty Images; cover, pp. 1–24 (background) Vadim Georgiev/Shutterstock.com; cover, pp. 1–24 (background) CS Stock/Shutterstock.com; p. 5 Nadezhda Bolotina/Shutterstock.com; p. 7 (main) Sergey Krasnoshchokov/Shutterstock.com; p. 7 (hollow hair) Scimat Scimat/Science Source/Getty Images; p. 7 (hoof) BMJ/Shutterstock.com; p. 9 Michio Hoshino/Minden Pictures/Getty Images; p. 11 V. Belov/Shutterstock.com; p. 13 (map) Serban Bogdan/Shutterstock.com; p. 13 (caribou) eyeCatchLight Photography/Shutterstock.com; p. 17 John E Marriott/All Canada Photos/Getty Images; p. 19 Timothy Fadek/Corbis News/Getty Images; p. 21 Terence Mendoza/Shutterstock.com.

Printed in the United States of America

CPSIA compliance information: Batch #CS18GS: For further information contact Gareth Stevens, New York, New York at 1-800-542-2595.

# CONTENTS

WORDS IN THE GLOSSARY APPEAR IN **BOLD** TYPE
THE FIRST TIME THEY ARE USED IN THE TEXT.

# Reindeer or CARIBOU?

If you've heard of reindeer, then you've heard of caribou! They're the same **mammal**, eating plants, living in herds in the cold North, and always moving to find food.

Today, there are about 5 million caribou. In North America, caribou live in herds throughout Canada and Alaska. There is only one species, or kind, of caribou. There are nine types of caribou within that species. Some types have already died out. Others, like the woodland caribou, are in danger of dying out. Weather, roads, and more can affect caribou.

> **THERE'S MORE!**
>
> CARIBOU EAT **LICHENS** (LY-kuhnz), GRASSES, MOSSES, AND OTHER GROUND PLANTS. WHEN THERE'S SNOW ON THE GROUND, THEY USE THEIR HOOFS TO DIG FOR FOOD!

lichens

# CREATURES!

Like most mammals, caribou give birth to live young, called calves. Caribou mothers, called cows, feed their calves milk from their body. Cows and calves know each other by smell, a caribou's strongest sense.

Caribou also have fur like other mammals. They have outer fur and underfur. Their outer fur is made up of hairs that are hollow. It traps heat and keeps the caribou warm. It also helps caribou float when they're swimming!

> ### THERE'S MORE!
>
> CARIBOU HOOFS HAVE SHARP EDGES FOR DIGGING IN SNOW FOR FOOD. PLUS, THEIR FEET ARE WIDE, ACTING AS PADDLES IN WATER AND **SNOWSHOES** IN DEEP SNOW.

hollow hair

hoofs

7

# MOVING

Some animals live in one place their whole life, but not caribou! Caribou herds migrate, or move every year as seasons change.

A herd's movement is based on where it lives, where it gives birth, and how many caribou it has. Some herds have 500,000 caribou! Sometimes different herds share an area for a winter season, but no herds give birth in the same place. That means scientists know which herd is which by where it gives birth!

> ## THERE'S MORE!
>
> CARIBOU HERDS HAVE SEVERAL PATHS THEY TAKE TO AND FROM WHERE THEY GIVE BIRTH, AND IT'S NEVER A STRAIGHT LINE! THEY CHOOSE A PATH BASED ON FOOD AND WEATHER.

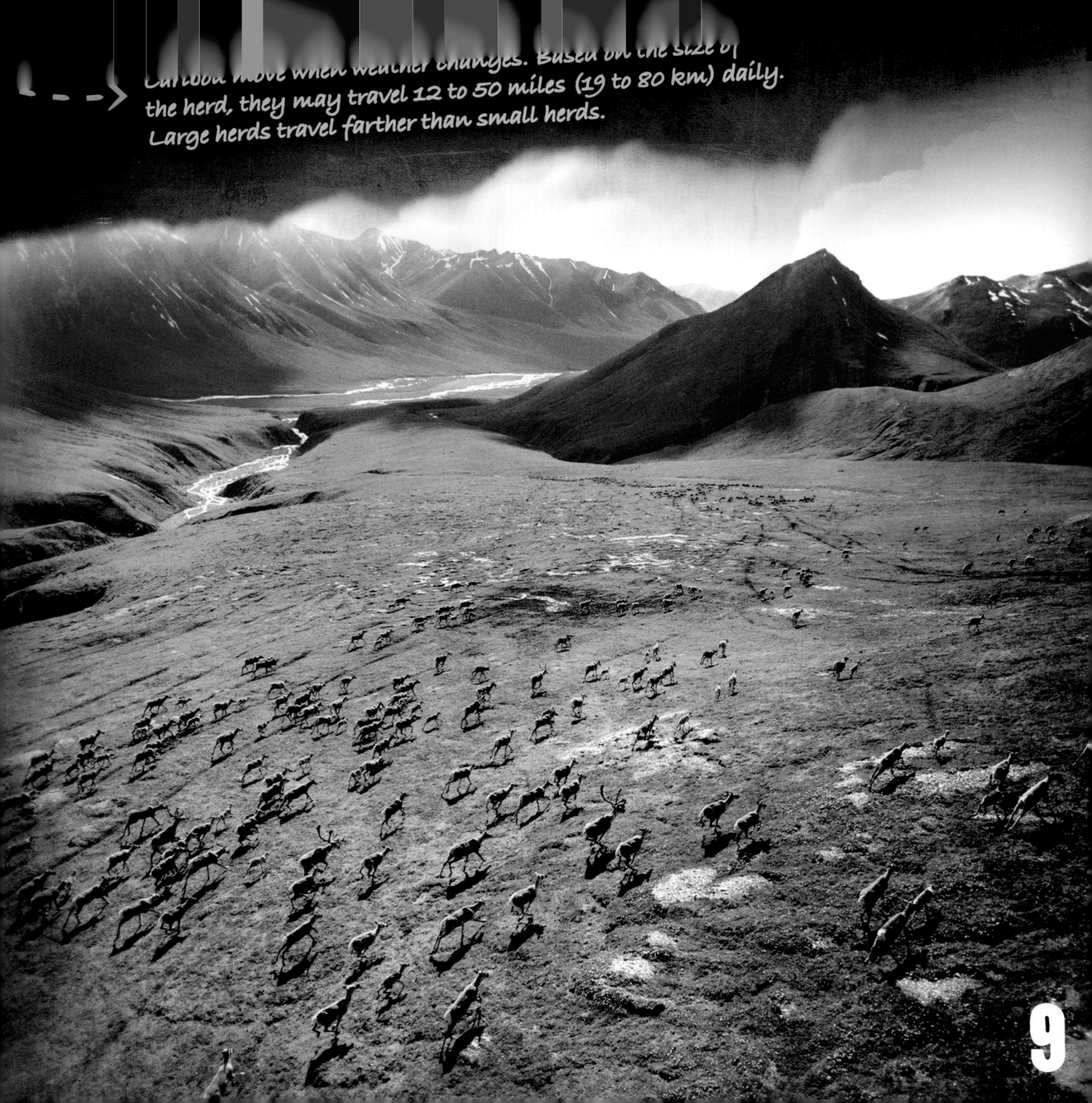

Caribou move when weather changes. Based on the size of the herd, they may travel 12 to 50 miles (19 to 80 km) daily. Large herds travel farther than small herds.

9

# The Caribou CALENDAR

Caribou **mate** in fall. In winter, they live where there's little snow so they can find food. Then herds break into groups to migrate to birthing areas in spring. Cows and young caribou travel first. Each group takes a different path so it's okay if the group ahead eats a lot!

Calves are born in late spring in a place with lots of **nutritious** plants, which help the mothers produce rich milk. Calves grow quickly so they can keep up with the summer migration when their herd comes together again.

THERE'S MORE!

GROWING QUICKLY MEANS CALVES CAN RUN TO ESCAPE PREDATORS AND BUGS. CARIBOU HATE BUGS AND WILL RUN AROUND TO AVOID THEM. THIS MAKES THEM LOSE WEIGHT NEEDED FOR WINTER!

Though they begin to eat ground plants 4 weeks after being born, caribou calves keep drinking their mother's milk for several months to grow quickly.

# A Special HERD

Porcupine caribou are a special herd named after a river in their range. They have the widest range of any land mammal in North America. They've been covering that 97,000-square-mile (250,000 sq km) range for 27,000 years!

Their range is wide because they **graze** in different areas from year to year to give each area time to regrow. That's because one Porcupine caribou eats almost 7 pounds (3 kg) of plants a day—even in winter!

## THERE'S MORE!

THE PLANTS FOUND IN WINTER AREN'T AS NUTRITIOUS. THEY'RE ALSO HARDER FOR CARIBOU BODIES TO HANDLE. EVEN SO, SOME CARIBOU GAIN WEIGHT IN WINTER BECAUSE THEY MOVE LESS BUT STILL EAT WELL!

ALASKA

CANADA

Porcupine
caribou range

13

# Porcupine Caribou MIGRATION

Porcupine caribou migrate among several different kinds of **habitats.** This means they're very good at **adapting** to food and weather changes, though some kinds of caribou aren't. Like other caribou, they migrate to give birth and find food. Their large, special migration is how they've survived for thousands of years in the harsh, cold North.

The Porcupine caribou's spring migration is very long and hard. But, it's worth it for the nutritious food and lack of predators and bugs at their birthing area.

## THERE'S MORE!

THE PORCUPINE CARIBOU'S BIRTHING LOCATION IS TOO COLD IN FALL AND WINTER FOR THEM TO STAY THERE. MIGRATION IS HARD, THOUGH, AND THEY HAVE MANY PREDATORS. ONLY HALF THEIR CALVES SURVIVE THEIR FIRST YEAR.

# THE PORCUPINE CARIBOU MIGRATION

**OCTOBER 8–NOVEMBER 30**

bulls, or males, fight over cows;
bulls and cows mate

DISTANCE: AROUND 200 MILES (320 KM)

**DECEMBER 1–MARCH 31**

move around winter area
searching for food

DISTANCE: A FEW HUNDRED MILES DEPENDING ON SNOWFALL

**APRIL AND MAY**

spring migration

DISTANCE: OVER 300 MILES (500 KM)

**JUNE 1–10**

cows move to
birthing areas

DISTANCE: AROUND 120 MILES (200 KM)

**JUNE 10–JULY 15**

cows and calves move
to avoid bugs

DISTANCE: AROUND 200 MILES (320 KM)

**JULY 16–AUGUST 7**

herd breaks into groups
because of food and bugs

DISTANCE: OVER 300 MILES (500 KM)

**AUGUST 8–OCTOBER 7**

fall migration south moves slowly
unless there's bad weather

DISTANCE: AROUND 250 MILES (400 KM)

15

# CARIBOU

Woodland caribou are a type of caribou that live in small herds in Idaho, Washington, and Montana. They used to live in forests all across the northern United States, in every state from the East Coast to the West Coast.

But today, their herds are small, and they aren't adapted to long migrations. In fact, they may migrate less than 40 miles (64 km) between summer and winter areas! Woodland caribou have lost much of their range to homes, roads, and mines. As their range becomes smaller, their numbers drop.

Woodland caribou haven't adapted like the Porcupine caribou have, so they're dying out. They may even be gone in your lifetime if something isn't done to help them!

17

# Western
# ARCTIC HERD

The Western Arctic herd is one of the largest caribou herds in the world—and maybe even one of the largest mammal herds! They live throughout 157,000 square miles (407,000 sq km) in northwest Alaska.

The Western Arctic herd's **population** has gone up and down a lot over the past 50 years. The herd's such an important part of Alaska's food web that scientists watch it closely. In 2016, the Western Arctic herd looked well fed and healthy.

## THERE'S MORE!

THE WESTERN ARCTIC HERD KNOWS WHEN TO MIGRATE BECAUSE OF CHANGING WEATHER AND CHANGES IN THE AMOUNT OF SUNLIGHT IN A DAY. IN FALL, ONLY SOME MOVE ON TO THE WINTER AREA.

To find out how many caribou are in a herd, scientists fly over herds as they migrate and take pictures. Then they count the number of caribou in their pictures.

19

# Staying ALIVE

Caribou don't have it easy. They're the main source of food for wolves in winter and grizzly bears in summer and winter. Many calves die in their first year. Cows have a new calf every year to keep their herd strong.

**Climate change** has brought thick ice that stops them from eating, heavy snows that stop migrations, and more bugs than ever. As new animals come from the South, new illnesses and predators fill caribou ranges. Hopefully, these wonderful creatures can survive all these changes!

> **THERE'S MORE!**
>
> CLIMATE CHANGE ALSO AFFECTS MIGRATION TIMING. CALVES ARE BORN TOO LATE FOR THE GOOD FOOD. CARIBOU HAVE TO SEARCH FARTHER AND FARTHER FOR FOOD.

The populations of 34 of the 43 major herds scientists study worldwide are getting smaller.

# GLOSSARY

**adapt:** to change to suit conditions

**climate change:** long-term change in the weather patterns of Earth, caused partly by people burning oil and natural gas

**graze:** to eat grass or other plants that are growing in a field at many times during the day

**habitat:** the natural place where an animal or plant lives

**lichen:** a plantlike living thing that grows on rocks and trees

**mammal:** a warm-blooded animal that has a backbone and hair, breathes air, and feeds milk to its young

**mate:** to come together to make babies

**nutritious:** advancing growth

**population:** a group of people or animals of one kind that live in a place

**snowshoe:** a frame attached to the foot and used to walk on deep or soft snow without sinking in

# FOR MORE INFORMATION

## Books

Hirsch, Rebecca, and Maria Koran. *Caribou: A Tundra Journey*. New York, NY: AV2 by Weigl, 2017.

Holing, Dwight. *Incredible Journeys: Amazing Animal Migrations*. New York, NY: Kingfisher, 2011.

Miller, Debbie S. *A Caribou Journey*. Fairbanks, AK: University of Alaska Press, 2010.

## Websites

**Caribou**
*nationalgeographic.com/animals/mammals/c/caribou*
Read interesting information about the caribou.

**Caribou**
*www.adfg.alaska.gov/index.cfm?adfg=caribou.video*
Watch this half-hour video about how scientists help caribou and brown bears in Alaska.

# INDEX